I0019051

The Future of Software Engineering:
Panel Discussions

22–23 November 2010, ETH Zurich

Transcribed and edited
by Edgar G. Daylight and Sebastian Nanz

Edgar G. Daylight is a postdoctoral researcher in the History of Computing, Eindhoven University of Technology, the Netherlands.

Sebastian Nanz is a postdoctoral researcher at the Chair of Software Engineering, ETH Zurich, Switzerland.
Contact: nanz@inf.ethz.ch

LONELY SCHOLAR™
SCIENTIFIC BOOKS

© 2011 Karel Van Oudheusden and Sebastian Nanz
Cover design © 2011 Kurt De Grave

Published by Lonely Scholar bvba
Sint-Lambertusstraat 3
3001 Heverlee
Belgium
editor@lonelyscholar.com
http://www.lonelyscholar.com

All rights reserved. No part of the publication may be reproduced in any form by print, photoprint, microfilm, electronically, or any other means without written permission from the publisher.

Alle rechten voorbehouden. Niets uit deze uitgave mag worden vermenigvuldigd en/of openbaar gemaakt worden door middel van druk, fotocopie, microfilm, elektronisch of op welke andere wijze ook zonder voorafgaande schriftelijke toestemming van de uitgever.

D/2011/12.695/2
ISBN 9789491386015
ISSN 2034-5976

Panel 1

Session Chair: Rustan Leino

Panelists:

- Barry Boehm
- Manfred Broy
- Erich Gamma
- Michael A. Jackson
- David L. Parnas
- Niklaus Wirth
- Pamela Zave

Leino: Good afternoon everyone. My name is Rustan Leino. I am going to be chairing this panel session, which is going to be mostly a question & answer session. I've been asked to give the speakers just a few minutes first to say any opening words that they care to. They may also pass since they have been speaking for 45 minutes to begin with[1]. For any

---

[1]The papers corresponding to the talks that were given by the panelists are collected in: Sebastian Nanz (ed.). *The Future of Software Engineering.*

1

opening statement you'd like to make you can have, let's say, about three minutes because we will have lots of discussion. Michael Jackson is put here on the spot first. So go ahead.

Jackson: I'll pass.

Leino: Okay, that's easy enough. We have gained three minutes. Niklaus Wirth?

Wirth: I have just been speaking, so I am waiting for questions. [Laughter]

Leino: We are in a time-saving mode. David Parnas?

Parnas: Well, I wanted to make a few remarks about the danger of learning about engineering from books that are written about engineers for people who are not engineers. We wouldn't want to read the books that are written about computers for people who are not computer scientists and actually believe them. Engineering specialization, Michael [Jackson], comes after graduation, not before. Some of the biggest breakthroughs in engineering, if you look closely at them, are done by people who transfer ideas from one specialty to another one. Such transfers are only possible because of the common basis. There are many breakthroughs in these transfers that you would never see in the superficial books written for public consumption. One of the things you said was that the Narrows bridge[2] was taught to all engineers and then you said that it was only about suspension bridges. In fact, the Narrows bridge is even taught to electrical engineers and to many other engineers because it is a lesson about proper use of models and understanding mathematical analysis. Just as the Comet[3] is not a lesson about windows, not even Microsoft

---

Springer, 2011. Additionally, slides and recordings of the talks are available on http://fose.ethz.ch/.

[2]The Tacoma Narrows Bridge, which collapsed soon after opening in 1940 due to forced resonance caused by winds of a certain speed.

[3]The de Havilland DH 106 Comet, one of the first jet airliners. The Comet suffered two catastrophic accidents in 1954, which were in part due to the square shape of its windows (metal fatigue cracks started in the window corners). The analysis of the accidents provided important lessons for all aircraft manufacturers.

Windows. The Comet was a lesson about not doing the proper analysis. It's a much more general lesson. The distinction that some books make between normal and radical — normal and radical implies that first you do radical and then comes a lot of normal engineering. In fact, if you look at the products, it is inter-mixed. There will be some radical and then there will be lots of little radical steps in between some normal copy-cat kind of models. The distinction is therefore misleading. Because every engineer has to do a bit of both to different degrees. It's also not true that engineers in software or engineers in any field can take other people's work for granted. They are in fact required by the laws in the various countries that licensed engineers to check everything and to make sure that their product will be fit for use. One of the big problems I have heard from industry is about software engineers that cannot talk to other engineers and it turns out to be because they are not engineers. They don't have enough in common with the other engineers to be able to understand what the other engineers are all about. This is the reason why in the recent things that I write about engineering I don't talk about software engineering any more. I talk about software-intensive engineering because I think this is what we should be teaching. We should be taking engineers and then letting them specialize late in their education in software-intensive systems.

I really didn't have much to object to Manfred Broy's talk except his idea of a list of requirements, because I don't think requirements are discrete entities and that you can count them or list them. I think basically a requirements document has to be a predicate and you can't in any way decide how many elements there are in a predicate, because there are many ways of writing it and each way gives you a different count.

I guess the only other thought I had — and I wanted to say this publicly because the man isn't here to defend himself. I agree to almost everything Niklaus Wirth said but I thought he wasn't fair to Bob Floyd. I have in fact promised to send him a copy of Bob Floyd's paper, because Bob Floyd's paper was not vague. It was very precise and was actually more precise and in some ways sounder than the papers that followed it for a while.

Broy: I'm not sure whether you are talking about the same paper.

Parnas: The 1968 [1967] paper 'Assigning Meanings to Programs'[4].

Broy: Is this what you [Wirth] were talking about?

Wirth: I was referring to the paper that appeared in 1968.

Parnas: I think that was the same one and I think that's the one Tony Hoare references. It was published twice. First in some conference and then in a mathematical journal, but it's the same paper in both cases.

Leino: Okay, thank you very much. Let's move on. Manfred Broy?

Broy: Of course I have to reply to what Dave Parnas said about requirements being one predicate or a list of requirements. Yes you are right and wrong at the same time. Unfortunately, it is very difficult to write such a large predicate in one step. So, practically, requirements are written by collecting requirements and in a certain sense people are interested then to understand this collection of requirements as one big predicate. And now there is the interesting logical question. If you understand requirements as logical properties, then you can do logical reasoning about those properties. Then you would find out that in practice most of the requirement collections you have are inconsistent. So there is no real predicate — it is just a predicate being inconsistent. Then you have to start to think about these different requirements and to ask yourself which of them is fine and which of them is not so fine. So, in the end, it boils down to looking at a

---

[4]Robert W. Floyd. Assigning meanings to programs. In: *Mathematical Aspects of Computer Science*, vol. 19 of Proceedings of Symposia in Applied Mathematics, pages 19–32. American Mathematical Society, 1967.

set of requirements. This is a difficult process because, as we know from a logical point of view, it does not matter how you cut a large predicate into small predicates (because the logic is always the same). Everything you derive from one you can derive from the other. But if you look at the concrete representation, it is different.

Parnas: What units are you measuring the size of your predicates in? Inches, meters, or what?

Broy: One thing is the size of the formulas.

Parnas: So it's the representation you are talking about.

Broy: Yes. Many people are bound to this expression.

I would like to say another thing about your relationship between the engineers and us. I work in a technical university and we have of course large engineering disciplines like electrical engineering and mechanical engineering. My feeling is that it is different to what you say. Nowadays we have a kind of convergence between working styles — I do not call it engineering for a moment — working styles you find in software development and working styles you find in the classical engineering disciplines. I'll give you some numbers, and I'm not claiming these numbers are absolutely right but they show you what's happening. **A.T. Kearney**[5] did a study on how the disciplines involved in the automotive field will develop over the years. Today software is about 15% of a car. Electronics is about 30% of a car and the rest is mechanics. Within the next 15 years, the software part will double, the electronic (hardware) part will stay the same, and the mechanical part will shrink by the amount the software will increase.

Zave: What was the unit?

Broy: The units were simply cost. I am not saying this is a very good measurement, but it shows what is going on. And I observe that these other engineering disciplines start to

---

[5] A management consulting firm.

change a lot, according to that. I speak about the step into systems engineering where you have to bring together software engineering issues with engineering practices from the classical disciplines. I found that very very interesting because it means also engineering will change a lot. So my view is different. I don't think that we have only to take over from the engineering disciplines — yes we have to — but on the other hand they have to, also. I think what is coming out is a kind of a merger.

Leino: Thank you very much. So we are going more into software-intensive engineering and it's becoming more important. Pamela Zave, do you care to say anything?

Zave: Well, David Parnas didn't make any complaints about my talk so I can pass. [Laughter]

Gamma: So maybe it's not a complaint but I must confess that the slide of Niklaus Wirth [in his talk] about good design was very intriguing to me. I noticed how I always reacted "but". I think it's really great to get this assessment from a neutral point of view. I just want to say some of my "buts" and constrain them to three. So, good examples to look at good designs. I think what I find very intriguing is that we now have open source, which means tons of opportunities to look at good source code. I get this one warm fuzzy feeling often when I read good source code. Yes, there are lots of curly brackets in there, but still I see that the community works together and it works well. So that's why I also encourage to work on an open-source project. If you don't work on it, read the code. It's helpful. You cannot do enough code reading the same way you can do book reading. The other "but" was about how you learn good design. I think what I found intriguing there is pair programming. When I pair program we can back check, I find it a great way to improve your design skill. Because you always learn from someone else. No matter whom I pair with, I learn something new. So, I think pair-wise programming is something that should be encouraged to students to improve their design skills and get better at it. And last but not least, the plea for feedback:

tools and so on. We have worked a lot on tools. I think these days the tools have succeeded in two areas: they allow for fast feedback and they allow me to make changes fast. This is what gives me comfort in improving my design. If I get feedback I know when I change something where I am. So I think there's still progress that I would like to emphasize here and encourage people to appreciate it. Once you have unit tests, once you have this red-green indication with fast turn-around, once you have refactoring tools, you can really start to move fast and be aggressive when it comes to improving your code. Those were my three "buts".

Leino: So, read code, code reuse, and pair programming.

Gamma: Continuous pair programming, continuous code reuse.

Leino: Great. Okay, Barry Boehm?

Boehm: People have asked about the timeless principles and I brought up the paper that has them here. This was a paper that was the keynote address at ICSE 2006 that was looking at the history of software engineering. In the 50s it was basically do software like you do hardware. The good lessons from that are don't neglect the sciences. This is the first part of the definition of engineering. It should not include just mathematics and computer science but also behavioral sciences, economics, and management sciences. It should also include using the scientific method to learn to experience. Another thing the hardware people do well is to measure twice and cut once which I translated into look before you leap, premature commitments can be disastrous. A negative thing is avoid using a rigorous sequential process; the world is getting too changeable and unpredictable for this and it is usually slower. From the 60s people were really doing artistic creative hacking. Positives about that were thinking outside the box, repetitive engineering would never have created the ARPANET or Engelbart's mouse and Windows' GUI. Have some fun prototyping, it is generally low risk and frequently high reward. Respect software's differences, you can't speed up its development indefinitely and since it is invisible you need to find good ways to make it visible and meaningful to different stake holders. The negative: avoid cowboy programming. So the last minute all night frequently does not work and the patchings get ugly fast. In the 70s, basically, people were sort of reconciling formality and agility. Well, more looking at requirements and specifications: eliminate errors early. Even better, prevent them in the future via root-cause analysis. Determine the system's purpose. Without a clear shared vision you are likely to get chaos and disappointment. All-question metric is another version of this. The negative was avoid top-down development and reductionism. COTS[6], reuse, I'll Know It When I See It, rapid changes and emergent requirements make this increasingly unrealistic for most applications. The 80s was a lot of emphasis on productivity. There are many roads to increase productivity, including staffing, training, tools, reuse, process improvement, prototyping and others. Another thing that happened in the 80s was Lee Osterweil's 'Software Processes Are Software Too'[7]. What's good for products is good for processes, including process architecture, process reusability, process composability, and adaptability. Another thing that happened in the 80s was Fred Brooks's 'Silver Bullet' paper[8]. Be sceptical about silver bullets and one-size-fits-all solutions.

Leino: Much good advice through the years. So, we are going to take Michael Jackson and then we are going to open up to the floor.

Jackson: Yes, passing on the first round I hope doesn't mean we're not allowed to say something on the second round.

Parnas: I hope not.

---

[6]Commercial-off-the-shelf software.

[7]Leon J. Osterweil. Software processes are software too. In: *Proceedings of the 9th International Conference on Software Engineering (ICSE'87)*, pages 2–13. ACM Press, 1987.

[8]Frederick P. Brooks. No silver bullet: Essence and accidents of software engineering. *IEEE Computer 20(4):10–19*, 1987.

Jackson: I've known Dave Parnas a long time. But, even after many many many years, I was quite unprepared for that. If I had imagined he would have spoken like that, I would have gone and sat over there [on the other side of the table] and then I would have been after him. Thank you [Leino] for giving me the chance to respond. Let me just take four things Dave said. He accused me of saying that you should take the work of others for granted. I said nothing of that sort. What I said was that if you want to distinguish software engineering as a part of system engineering, then you can think of it as that part in which you do not make changes to the problem world. That does not mean that you don't have to analyze it. It does not mean you don't have to consider failures of designed engineered systems. It does not mean you don't have to consider failures of trained operators and so on. So I think that was a misunderstanding. As for the question about specialization and general education, I did actually say specifically, if David had been listening, that I had been told by him before, not that I didn't know it, that there were general principles, and of course those were shared by specialists of various kinds. Vincenti — I asked Dave earlier today whether he had read this book[9]. And his answer was: "I looked at it but it was boring". That was what he said. If he had read it, he might have found that it is not at all a boring book and, in particular, that it makes the point which I thought was implicit in my talk, which is that in any real project there are certainly going to be elements that are radical as well as elements that are normal. Karl Benz was actually an engineer who had done various things, including bicycles and you can even see some of the effects of that in his cars' designs. So there is a mixture of radical and normal engineering. You can make a radical composition of normal parts. You can introduce new radical parts into a normal design as when you introduce automatic gear boxes into motorcars, and so on and so forth. So, my suggestion

---

[9]Walter G. Vincenti. *What Engineers Know and How They Know It: Analytical Studies from Aeronautical History*. Johns Hopkins University Press, 1990.

to Dave is that he just listen a little bit more carefully next time. [Laughter]

Parnas: And I will hear things that he didn't say the first time.

Jackson: And read Vincenti.

Parnas: Not worth the time.

Jackson: Dave says "It's not worth the time". He hasn't read it but he knows it's not worth the time. May I suggest that any of you who are interested should look at this book. It is well worth your time.

Leino: Thank you. Great, now we would like to open up to questions from the audience. Bertrand Meyer?

Bertrand Meyer: I have a question for David Parnas. First I would like to thank you for your outstanding talk. I really don't want to offend anyone, but for me you are really the best speaker to disagree with. [Laughter] I have an impolite question and a technical one. I'll start with the impolite question. When I was growing up, there were these papers by a guy — whose name just escapes me for the moment — about information hiding and such matters, which really taught me that I had to worry a lot in software about change. A way to protect myself against change was to separate the specification from the implementation. Then there were these papers by some other guy — actually it may have been the same guy, I forgot — which talked about designing software for change. And now I come here and my eyesight is not that good so there is some person who I vaguely see in the back who is saying that we should have the code and then we should have documentation and they absolutely have to be different products. In particular, you shouldn't even think about extracting the documentation from the code. This is like bridges, right? But actually in my experience, software is very different from bridges, although I must admit that I have much more experience with software than with bridges, except as a user. One of the main problems I learned with software is that it changes. So if you have that the documentation is so important as a separate product, of course the day that the documentation exists it is already lying, it is already different from the software. My question is how do you address this fundamental Dorian-Gray phenomenon of software development?

Parnas: The same principles that allow you to design software for change allow you to design documents for change. So, for example, the way we documented the inspection of the Darlington Nuclear Plant, when changes were necessary they resulted in very small changes to the corresponding documentation and the rest of the documentation was provably not necessarily changed. That's a matter of structuring the documentation. Design for change extends to both the software itself and the documents.

Leino: Okay, next question.

Anonymous: I have a continuation to the previous question. It's really hard to keep the documentation and the code in sync, because code changes every day and hardly any developer would change documentation every day — at least the ones I know. So, isn't it necessary for this documentation, to really work, to be executable and verifiable?

Parnas: I think it's important that it's not executable but that it be interpretable. The difference is that each of the documents that I talk about is actually a predicate and, for example, we can take them and translate them into — excuse me [directed to Wirth] — a C program [Laughter]. Any programming language, but we happen to use C — a C program that would be usable as a test oracle. So one of the things it imposes on people who use this method is when they change the code, they also change the documentation, because the documentation is used to test the code.

Leino: Manfred, you are going to follow up on that?

Broy: A side remark. I told Dave Parnas several times that I don't think documentation is a good term for what he is doing. We would rather talk about artifact models. Documentation, at least in my understanding, is a little bit after the fact. For me it is interesting to do the forward engineering by working out useful artifacts, and I agree completely, it is a good idea to have artifacts which are to such an extent formal so that you can do tool work with them. I know of at least one company which does not write a line of code any more. They just write down the artifacts at a modelling level, and do all the code generation and document generation from the artifacts. Then this being in sync is solved by generating the information from the same artifacts.

Parnas: There is a large class of programs where if you have what we call a program-function table, you can generate the code automatically. Those aren't the interesting programs though. Those are fairly dull programs. But I think you need to correct one thing. If you look at the way that several engineers use documentation, it is not after the fact. Each document is finished, signed off, and used as a basis for the next step. So it is during the process and before each next step that it becomes important.

Wirth: Just a comment about your mentioning of C [directed to Parnas]. Everybody gets the language that he deserves. [Laughter]

Leino: Next question.

Yuri Gurevich: A lot was said that, in software engineering, we should follow the example of traditional engineering. I think this is overdoing it a little bit. It seems to me that the notion of engineering changes; it becomes wider and wider; it acquires new branches, software engineering being one, bio engineering being another. These are radically different from traditional engineering and certainly they require new mathematics — nobody argues with this in bio engineering. I think it's very easy to make a case that you need new mathematics, new logic, new specification languages and so on for these new branches of engineering.

Leino: Does any one want to comment on this?

Parnas: I want to comment on that. I think we are in danger of descending to a debate about words. But I consider the two examples you gave as an abuse of the language. Many people use the word "engineering" in a way that it means nothing more than "building". To me, as a trained and licensed engineer, it means a lot more than building. I don't know many properly trained software engineers, and the bio engineering that I have seen is not engineering at all. It's just constructive use of biology.

Boehm: I guess I'd like to put in a plug for the users and considering them when doing not just user interfaces but documentation. I look at the help messages I get from software products. I look at the user's manual I get from my cell phone and they look like they were written for programmers by programmers. So, I think the kind of documentation, Dave Parnas, that you are doing is necessary but not sufficient.

Parnas: I think I even had a slide that said that. And in fact I think if we did better professional documentation, we would be then free to have documentation just for the user. And not all the users are the same, there are some engineers who use cell phones.

Jackson: Could I just add a little anecdote about user interfaces. We recently stayed in an apartment of a friend for three months and the clock on the oven was set to the wrong time so I wanted to reset it. Well it subsequently turned out that one of the buttons was stuck on, but that was actually, as it turned out, the reason why I was completely unable to reset the clock. I went to the source of all wisdom in these circumstances, which is `Google`, and I put in "set clock timer X" with X being the model of the oven. And `Google` produced pages and pages and pages and pages of results saying how to set the clock on the `Westinghouse` this and the `Siemens` that. It was just splendid, I was delighted. It is obvious that no one who has designed the software for these ovens has ever made that inquiry of `Google`.

Leino: Okay, next question.

Anonymous: I have a question about Professor Wirth's remark [in his talk] about the `Verilog` compiler's messages. I suspect, like in many other cases, that the people who wrote the compiler are not really software engineers. I think in practice there are lots of people writing software who are maybe even called software engineers but they are not really specialized in software engineering. In fact some of you argued for having specializations, so people specialized in even different areas of computer science, but not really studying anything about computer science. So, I think this is a problem in practice, no matter how many researchers and educators we have that talk about software engineering, this doesn't really reach the practicing engineers who create the software.

Wirth: You are probably right. The interesting parts in the `Verilog` system are of course those which do generate the circuits and the layouts, and the optimization of the circuits, and not necessarily just the user interface and the syntax checking front. But you may be right. I'm sure that system was written 20 years ago, at least the beginnings of it. But it's still bad for the year 2010!

Broy: I think we have to be careful to see that software is not equal to software. We have such a rich variety of software systems. And, of course, it is a different situation if Niklaus Wirth is working on his own and having some ideas of what to do and trying to do some constructions. I'm not even sure that I would call that software engineering because that's much closer to programming and trying things out and so on, which is a fine thing to do. My feeling is that software engineering is much more challenging in a situation where you have a large team, where you have diverging interests, different stake holders, and you have to bring things together. And I am completely with Barry Boehm what he was talking about: then management is a big issue. At least I've seen a number of software projects that did not fail according to technicalities, not according to the fact that they couldn't specify properly or they couldn't do the good design properly.

But there was a lot of fighting going on between different stake holders and the executive management had no idea what software was about. I know of a number of ridiculous management decisions. I give you one, which is absolutely true, a large project was late in time and then the big boss was flying in and talking to the project members what to do. They showed him their plans, how to do the project. And he looked at that and said "oh, you plan to spend a lot of time on module tests, that takes most of your time, so just skip them". And he went away again and they skipped module tests. And the project crashed. So, in a certain sense, I think there are so many things to take care of. It's management, it's bringing people together, it's having people at different sites and coordinating them, and then in the end coding is just a small part of it. How much of it would really go into coding? In a certain sense, Erich Gamma was talking about software being just the code, but that's not correct. Software is much more than just the code. I think one of the big issues is what are the artifacts you need in addition to the code. We do a lot of code inspections. If we have a real good project which takes care of software quality for which we look at the code, we could be much better in trying to understand the quality of software if we had more information. For instance, what I am missing completely in all these current programming languages is architecture information. Where do you express architecture information in your programming language? If you are interested to read about that, we just published an article in IEEE. We had a workshop a year ago where we tried to understand this issue better. I would even go beyond what Niklaus Wirth is saying. It's not just C, but I think a lot of the work on programming languages nearly stopped 15 years ago. And if you look at Java, they have forgotten some of the golden rules Niklaus Wirth introduced. Isn't that a pity? Actually I think we have to work hard at the language level to become better and then to be able to do more comprehensive designs — are current languages good for web design Pamela Zave? I don't think so. We are living in a concurrent world, we live in the reactive world. In ALGOL 60, input and output was not part of the language, because at that time it was not considered important. There we are.

Parnas: May I ask a simple question to Manfred Broy? Why do you believe that the architecture information has to be written in a programming language and be part of the code?

Broy: Very simple, because if you don't do that, it disappears, it vanishes over time. We have seen designs of helicopters where you cannot find back the architecture description that you find in some of your documentation.

Leino: Next question.

Egon Börger: My question is for Niklaus Wirth. I told you after your talk that I was delighted to hear that you define programming as designing abstract machines. But I think it shows also a problem, I mentioned to you the example which I find is a good example. It's your booklet of the 80s if I remember well where you start with a small pseudo-code text of six or eight lines of an interpreter for a sublanguage of Pascal, and after 90 pages you conclude with a complete compiler for that part of the language. But, in between, you never have a single Pascal program. You don't even have a program in any specific programming language. But you have what you call pseudo code or we could say nowadays abstract machines. So the problem this brings to me is the following: don't we need a language, because you said that from the point of view of a language we are fine today, but I disagree. Don't we need languages or a language which supports construction of abstract machines with as much good control and module structure and architectural parts which we need to have a full abstract description of a system, without going into all the details in which this part of the description is handled in different programming languages?

Wirth: Well, why don't you just use a subset, a small subset even, of the system's language for specifying this abstract machine?

Egon Börger: Which language? That was my question. Which language for abstract machines? Well, I favor one language but I don't want to mention that here.

Wirth: Which language? Well, to my mind, of course immediately comes `Oberon`, a subset of `Oberon`. You could well use that. We don't need another language.

Egon Börger: But you couldn't describe this beautiful transformation of your six lines of pseudo code to a `Pascal` compiler in `Oberon`, you couldn't. It's a different language, that's what I want to point out. But it's all about abstract machines, here I fully agree. Yuri Gurevich's definition of abstract state machines would cover your entire construction, but it lacks architectural features.

Wirth: I don't have that example in mind, so I can't answer the question definitely, but I would say most probably yes.

Leino: Alright, next question.

Jochen Ludewig: Talking about the future of software engineering, I wonder if we can expect any of the traditional problems that we have had now for decades will be solved or will at least be some way easier than they used to be. For instance, we still don't really know how to write a specification. We still don't know how to represent a design. We still don't know how to test software. Of course, we know a lot about these things, but there is no real philosophy of doing these things and also there are no text books containing large and convincing examples, at least to my knowledge. So, question to the whole panel, which problems will, can, could possibly be solved?

Zave: Well, you're right, there are a lot of techniques that have been proposed and researched and they are not used, not very much or enough. I think that the principle reason is that if you are working on a real software system, it is far far far too difficult to start from scratch and produce descriptions, specifications, and requirements of the completeness and detail that are needed. These are big problems in big software systems and it is far far too difficult to start from scratch, when you have a project to do. It seems to me that the only possible way to solve this problem is to have more emphasis on domain-specific modelling and on, essentially, building up the vocabulary and the artifacts for a particular domain, so that a project doesn't need to start from scratch. So that a new project can start with a big library of such artifacts for similar systems in that domain and then just modify them or use them for whatever is appropriate. That's the only way that I conceive of this ever working in practice.

Boehm: I have a couple of responses. One, as far as domain-specific approaches are concerned, there are a lot of success stories there where people have developed executable model definitions and you can model the control system for a satellite and execute the code for it. Similarly for other kinds of vehicles. The main way that they succeed is by making assumptions that short cut all the generality that you have. One of the big challenges is when you try to compose these together: we had a problem in the US defense department where the domain-specific model for the ground vehicles assumed the earth was flat and for the air vehicles they assumed it was spherical and for the satellites the assumption was that it was oblate, nobody knew where the objects were.

Zave: And that's exactly why we need an experience and an history of these things too. Because over time you can work out these problems.

Boehm: The other thing you can do is a sort of meta-modelling that helps you discover where these inconsistencies are.

Broy: I'm not sure whether you [directed to Jochen Ludewig] wanted to express what you sounded like expressing, namely that there's no progress. It's not true. There's a lot of difference if you look at different companies and different projects. I think one of the big problems is not just research progress, which is one thing, the other thing is the transfer progress. I've seen too many projects which make the same mistakes over and over again, they don't use the simple methods and principles which have already been found out by people like Dave Parnas over thirty years ago. So, I think the problem is very simple: a lot of people who deal with software don't understand what they are dealing with. Therefore, we have to distinguish between the state of research and the state of practice, and that's a big difference. Today, if you look for instance at `Google`, we did some quality checks within `Google` in the projects, and I think I understand now the quality of software within `Google`, and we did it within many other companies, and then you see a big spectrum of differences. So I think it's one side. I think software engineering is much better than people would believe when listening to this conference. Because we have a lot of software in operation, in particular in aircrafts, which is doing extremely fine. It is doing much better than in some of the other engineering disciplines. Dave Parnas, I am sorry to say that. On the other hand, there is a lot of software that is rubbish, it is done in a rubbish-style way. Therefore it is very difficult to speak about the field in general terms. I think we have to develop a much better understanding about how we rate the quality of software. I know Bertrand Meyer wanted to talk about one of the fellows who is responsible for the capability-maturity model [CMM] today or tomorrow. But CMM is only one way to look at it. It is a way to look at the software processes and perhaps also a rather bureaucratic way of doing it. We are interested also in understanding the quality of software and the quality of the artifacts related to software. If you do that, you'll find out that there are a lot of differences and we have to develop a kind of a systematics which allows us to call good software good software and bad software bad software, likewise for good design and bad design.

Gamma: I think one big help here is transparency into software. That's something we do and we learn from open source. Expose your code, expose your intermediate milestones to a community of users so that they can give feedback. You don't want to have the big boss come in at the end who says "skip module testing" because that's not incremental. You want to do things incrementally. To do that, you want to get transparency at intermediate steps. So I believe that transparency helps improve quality. Actually, even for our commercial software, we are fully transparent, you can see our bug tracks, you can see our milestones. We expose these things that we care about, which has two benefits. First of all, it is transparency to the customer, but it is also accountability from us as the development team. That's why transparency is the big weapon to make progress. Make it transparent where you are, and don't only make it available at the end, but make it available at incremental steps. I think that would make things visible, change will happen. If you don't make them visible, people will go into the dark and just continue with the way they always have been.

Parnas: I want to take what was said in reverse. First of all I would like to endorse something Manfred Broy said about we needing some standards to decide what is good or bad, because I was floored twice in the last five minutes, my mouth literally fell open and I had to really hold it up like that. Once when you [Gamma] said that open-source software was good, because every time I look I see crap.

Gamma: It's a spectrum, from happiness to unhappiness.

Parnas: I must have a way of picking up the crap, but I think maybe we need to find some agreed standard for judging it. Because I have looked at a lot of avionics software, I have looked at it very very closely, and I thought it was horrible. And, I just don't understand what you [Broy] makes you think it's fine. But, maybe it's German software that is fine, I don't know. What I really want to respond to, however, is Pamela Zave's repeating the often-heard myth that it is far too difficult to invest time in specifications. If you write the right specifications, they save time. And this has been shown in many projects. If you write VDM or Z, it is a waste of time. If you write a lot of those things, but if you write down the information that people need to decide before they write the code, the coding goes very fast. I don't think there is any basis for that myth that it is too difficult. The final thing that I wanted to say was to Jochen Ludewig. First of all, I think we don't want to solve these problems, we want to ameliorate them. That's the right word. Second, I want to ask you who was the "we" in "we all don't know"?

Jochen Ludewig: Well, if you like, I can exclude you. [Laughter]

Parnas: You can begin there, but you can't end there.

Leino: Alright, next question.

Mehmet Aksit: I would like to put attention to systemic properties of systems. What I mean is, since we are comparing everything with traditional engineering, so if you for example have an electronic amplifier, what is important there is, let's say, frequency bandwidth and harmonic distortion and amplification factor, maybe how much energy it dissipates and all these things. These are all systemic properties. And, of course, components there are important but it is important that all components work together. Mostly, engineers learn techniques to calculate frequency bandwidth from the properties of components. So, going from component specification to let's say system-wide properties which you may call architectural properties. And, so, Broy touched it a little bit. You could also refer to this as a way of composition refers to your incrementality but it's not trivial at all. I think this is a very important thing that we should be mastering. Going from systemic to components we have and the properties of systems that we want to design. Of course, design patters try to do that in microscopic scale. But, we don't really have that much understanding. Except that we do have excellent understanding of using them. But, still, it is a challenge if more than one pattern work together, and what does it mean and so forth. You may say that this is a trivial thing in logic, because logic can easily express compositions. In other words I call it a composition problem, what I just mentioned. But it's not easy. If you look at electronic amplifier, it is not a logical composition, many semantic issues are involved. Therefore, for me, to summarize, composition is the key.

Zave: I would like to respond to David Parnas's comment about the difficulty of specifications. I just want to clarify what I was talking about and certainly from the examples I have seen in David's talk, these are all specifications of programs whose boundaries are quite small and well defined. As you can see from my talk, I am concerned about networks and network services that are very important today, where there is a tremendous number of aspects involved and basically for none of them does anyone have any good idea of what the correct abstractions are. There is a tremendous need for abstractions and nobody knows what the right ones are. Without the right abstractions, we just drown in a sea of complexity. So, to clarify what I was talking about, working in such a domain, you have to figure out what nobody knows which is what are the right abstractions to make this domain comprehensible. You have to figure that out before you start your project. Maybe it would be cost effective to figure it out, but you just can't.

Parnas: Who's "you"?

Zave: The person whose job it is to develop the software. It seems to me very clear that in terms of domain-specific modeling (which is something I am very interested in) one of the big problems is that — I think most people I talk to are very in favor of it, but nobody takes responsibility for doing it. Typically, software researchers want to do things that are completely generic and apparently assume that the practitioners will apply their ideas. But, that's actually quite ludicrous because the practitioners don't have the time and they usually also don't have the right training or perspective or interest. They are not interested in that kind of work. It seems to me that it's the people who do research who basically have that kind of interest in looking for abstractions, but you know, they are not doing it. I see a real vacuum there.

Gamma: Interest is a real challenge here. If an engineer has an option between writing a library or a specification, I can tell you what I would do, I would write an implementation framework because that makes it fun and I can run it. So we need to get more specifications. So I guess you have to add additional guidance and goals so that specifications can be more encoded in an implementation framework. I have no good ways to do that but it's definitely a very interesting area where we have to push forward because that gives the decoupling that we want to achieve.

Broy: Pamela Zave you were talking about finding the right abstractions while you accused me [during the break] that my talk was too abstract. [Laughter] But, more seriously, I think, yes, this is exactly what I tried to talk about in my talk. That you have different abstractions in a development and that you have to understand how to relate these different abstractions. So you can choose the right abstraction for the purpose you are working on currently. Yes, I agree, just finding such theoretical insights doesn't make people in practical engineering use it. So the interesting question is how to do the transfer model. I'll just give you my view. We work a lot with certain industries and try out those things in real projects in industry and see to what extent it actually works out in practice. I think that's one way to do it. It is again the question of what is the difference between engineering with software-intensive systems and engineering in a situation where there is not a lot of software. If you look at the car industry, that was an assembly industry a few years ago. They just assembled things and the parts that they assembled did not have much to do with each other. You only needed a geometrical fitting for the parts, and other issues were not so important. Nowadays, it is completely different because you have a lot of dependencies there. You have many many functions which depend on each other. We are currently running a project with a car industry where they try to take over the software modeling technique we have developed for the other parts, because they think it is so important to understand that these parts are no longer just building blocks from a geometrical point of view but they have functionality. They want to develop what they call a functional view on their systems, which is not just the software, it is the whole system and the system parts. I think this is a very interesting and very fruitful way to bring things together and this is the only way to go, because in the future there will be no technical project without software in it. So we have to understand engineering as an engineering that includes mechanical, hardware, and software engineering side by side.

Boehm: As another response to Jochen Ludewig, addressing composability is much more complex for a COTS[6]-, cloud-, or legacy-intensive application than for a custom application. A lot of the applications that we see are applications concerning small businesses or community-service organizations or local governments. The economics drive them to put together such packages as a content-management system, a customer-relations management system, or a credit-card payment system. Basically, the COTS and cloud packges are not transparent. They are opaque, they are not things that you can precisely specify and reason about. You can't even fully define the process that you are going to use for the project. Your process begins by determining the best of the 40 candidate content management systems, the best of the 30 customer relations management systems, and so forth. And, once you determine them in step 1, you need to determine their shortfalls with respect to satisfying your system needs, and set up a step 2 to compensate for those. And you can't have an up-front Integrated Master Schedule, because you can't specify step 2 until you've done step 1.

Parnas: I want to be begin by saying that nobody responded to Mehmet Aksit's question except maybe a little bit Barry Boehm, but I don't agree with what he said. You are right when you say that in electrical circuits we use functional composition. The good news is that if you do software with the right approach, you are also using functional composition. In fact, if you watched Manfred Broy's slides carefully, his definition is exactly the definition of functional composition, expressed from a predicate point of view. You can always do that. The bad news is that the functions are no longer continuous but they are piecewise continuous. That means that you have to break it down to a lot of little compositions and do it in a systematic way which is one of the reasons the tabular notation is an advantage. However, it is still basically the same mathematics.

The other thing that I wanted to say is that I don't think anybody should judge a method by the examples that fit on slides. You [Pamela Zave] said you saw these little self-contained things. We've done for the old AT&T some examples and they were pages and pages. The nuclear plant was still done before PDF and was 45 kilograms, 90 pounds for you, of paper. These are not little examples and they are not done by researchers, they are done by trained disciplined engineers. I think what's missing when people keep saying nobody does this is that nobody is training those people. Nobody is showing those people how to do it, no manager is telling them that they have to do it. I think the real test for any method is what happens after you try it in the company. If people continue doing it after you leave, you've done right. If they don't continue doing it, as has happened in many many cases, then you've done wrong. That's what you have to look at. When I left that little Columbus AT&T lab, they did 14 more. Then the company got broken up, I don't know what happened after that. When I left the nuclear power people, they kept doing it, they are still doing it today. When I left the US Navy, to my great regret, they are still using it, and that's because I've become anti-navy. That's the measure to look for, and I don't think people are looking. I think we have very bad communication in this field.

Mehmet Aksit: Can I respond? I think it is not that easy as you formulated. I agree that logic gives us a nice formulation, I refer to actually Manfred Broy's talk, but if you look at the semantics of certain compositions or semantics of, let's say, patterns, it is not trivial at all to go systematically using compositional operators and analysis techniques to go from component behavior to systemic behavior. I think, still, that we are at the infancy. Especially if the properties cannot be hierarchically decomposed. Take, for example, availability characteristics. Or take, for example, performance. Take, for example, functional behavior for complex systems. So I think we are not yet there.

Parnas: I just want to point out that I did not say that it is trivial. What it actually is is tedious. It is incredibly tedious and this is why the idea of having researchers do it is wrong, because one thing researchers don't like is tedium.

Leino: Let's turn to Niklaus Wirth first and then we have a couple of questions from the floor.

Wirth: I would actually like to come back to an earlier statement made by Manfred Broy. He said that in German car manufacturers by now 15% of the cost goes into software and 30% into electronics. And the trend is increasing for software?

Broy: That's right.

Wirth: Somehow this seems to me a kind of a cyclic state of affairs. The question is what to do about it. There are basically two solutions. One is to increase the cost of the hardware, of the wheels of the motor and all this. And I think that is going to happen any way.

Broy: No.

Wirth: And the second is to lower the cost of the software. There are basically two ways of doing that. The first one is to switch to open software, because that's for free. The second is to reduce the cost of producing software and here I now become serious. I think indeed there is a lot of good software in the world: most of the things work most of the time. What we really criticize is that there are still some cases of bad software. Not that the whole state is bad but that we can do much better. And I particularly would like to say that we can do much better in cost effectiveness of programs, of utilization of the hardware facilities. That is where we should and can still make dramatic improvements.

Leino: Great. I am going to take two questions that have been in the queue for a while. So, let's take Bertrand Meyer first.

Bertrand Meyer: Actually I had a question on a different topic, which is related to Pamela Zave's talk. I want to ask this question even though it is a bit specific, because I do think that part of the future of software engineering is through the Internet and maybe the other way around as well. If we ignore Internet and web programming, we are not going to be very relevant. I was intrigued by this concept of overlay. I wonder, I cannot place this abstraction well, what is it? You presented it more as a networking concept, but since this is a software engineering conference, what does it mean from a software engineering viewpoint? Is it a design pattern? Is it a modular construct that we should add to the next programming languages? Is it a step in the software process?

Zave: As I said, it's definitely, I think, the correct module of network architecture. I think that the working hypothesis is that — it might not be true, but it looks good to me at the moment — a modular network architecture is not a collection of many completely different kinds of modules as some other architectures might be. But it's actually a repetition of different instances of this general pattern or template over different scopes, different levels of the hierarchy, and for different purposes. Now, it can certainly be described as a template or pattern. It's got a lot of moving parts, so that makes it more complex than probably most patterns. I am sure that you can fruitfully decompose it and look at separate things — certainly there is a whole world to say about routing algorithms, that's what networking is mostly about. There certainly is a whole lots of things to say about how to make a distributed directory and so forth. So it is a very complicated pattern. But the working hypothesis is that every overlay is some sort of specialization of this pattern. Does that answer your question?

Bertrand Meyer: Should it be a language construct?

Zave: Oh, I have no idea. I need to talk to a language designer about that.

Leino: And one last question in the back.

Anonymous: Many of the panel members have said this is good software and the other is crap. I would like to know if there is a consensus on what good is. Isn't that maybe one of the problems here? Maybe Erich Gamma with his design patterns has another connotation of what good or quality means, while maybe Manfred Broy working with software for airplanes looks at it differently. And maybe even in the same application domain, because you [Gamma] have also mentioned design patterns for real-time embedded systems on one of your slides. Is there actually a consensus on what good software is because if you don't have that, you are already stuck with a problem, right?

Broy: The answer is fairly simple. There are quality models. And quality models for software are quite large and they talk about quite different aspects of software quality. Though you couldn't say it is good or bad, you could say "if I take this quality model and if I try to evaluate the software according to the quality model, then you get out a quality profile" and we've done that many times and then you can compare. And, as I've said, if you have the same software, in more or less the same domain, then you have the quality profile, this allows you to really say this is a better software than the other one. If you are in completely different domains, you have different quality requirements and that makes a difference.

I would just like to say two sentences to what Niklaus Wirth was saying. It's not so much the question of the cost. Software brings so much difference to the cars, also benefits. I know the cars you drive and I drive are the same and they have changed a lot over the years. In the old winter time one of the rules of the cars we were driving was: put a heavy sandbag in the back of the car to make sure that if it's icy on the roads you are more safe. You don't need the sandbags any more. This is just one example of that. The next step is talking about electrical cars which will be completely different. We will get rid of a lot of the mechanical parts because it is electrical any how. You will have much more X-by-wire than you have today which will change the car completely. It's not just that the software gets more costly, it also offers much more. It would be interesting if you look at a car 30 years ago and today, it's a big difference. Another thing is, just to emphasize how important it is, we have much fewer people killed in accidents today, and it's due, to a large extent, to a lot of software in the cars.

Parnas: And seat belts.

Broy: And seat belts, which are by the way controlled by software.

Leino: There are several more questions. If you have more questions, hold them to dinner, ask them there, ask them tomorrow. Let's thank the panel.

Panel 2

Session Chair: Michael A. Jackson

Panelists:

- Patrick Cousot[10]

- Yuri Gurevich

- Rustan Leino

- Bertrand Meyer

- Andreas Zeller

Jackson: I'm going to ask each of the panelists in turn to take no
more than one minute to make no more than one comment
on one talk[11], the comment being intended to stimulate
discussion after all of the comments have been made. And
then I'll throw it open for more comments from the panelists

---

[10]Respecting Patrick Cousot's request not to transcribe his oral remarks,
the editors have paraphrased (in the form of footnotes) some of the points he
raised and which were taken up by other panelists.

[11]The papers corresponding to the talks that were given by the panelists
are collected in: Sebastian Nanz (ed.). *The Future of Software Engineering.*
Springer, 2011. Additionally, slides and recordings of the talks are available on
http://fose.ethz.ch/.

and from you with the proviso that nobody should make a speech or deliver a lecture because we have really a short amount of time. Rustan Leino, would you like to begin?

Leino: Sure. My comment is a question for Andreas Zeller. When languages will all have constructs for writing specifications (and in particular I'm thinking of preconditions) programmers will have the ability (the moment they think of the precondition) to express that in the language. Do you think that will reduce the need for mining specifications?

Jackson: Thank you Rustan Leino. Yuri Gurevich?

Gurevich: I have a comment on the last question that was posed after Andreas Zeller's talk, whether we need all that [i.e., technology to mine specifications] because in the future everybody would write specifications first and develop code from there. I think Andreas should have answered that there is a difference between future and utopia. [Laughter]

Zeller: My comment is not directed towards particular speakers. But, to quote Yuri, I sometimes feel that the assumption is made that we are already living in some kind of utopia: we are surrounded by super smart people who are not afraid of any kind of formalism, who are not afraid of reinventing everything there is already once again. And I wonder how our own discipline will connect, not to utopia, but to real-life programmers who will have to integrate all these new techniques into their daily lives at some point.

Jackson: Thank you Andreas Zeller. Bertrand Meyer?

Meyer: I just gave a talk, so I'll pass.

Jackson: Before I throw it open to the floor, Andreas Zeller, would you like to answer the questions that were posed to you?

Zeller: Let me try to answer all three questions. First Rustan Leino. You've been asking whether our programming languages should be designed in a way to better integrate abstractions, specifications, and everything. Actually I think that our programming languages, as we have them right now, are almost irresponsible in the way that they only address low-level issues. Actually I find it a total scandal that, say, something like the *assert* keyword has taken years and years until it made it into Java. As far as I understand it, it is the least used keyword of all, which is a scandal to me. I think we should be able to express what we want to do at many different levels of abstraction, coming from the highest level to the lowest level, and merging of course all these abstractions as they are being specified for all sorts of verification.

Speaking to Yuri Gurevich about your question of utopia. Are we talking about the future, are we talking about some utopia? And also responding to Patrick Cousot at this point, I think we need to be ambitious[12]. I think it's important to have a vision of what the future should look like. It's important to have an utopia in mind, this is important for any kind of science. It's important to know what we want to achieve, it's important to know where we want to go. Of course, an utopia by definition is unreachable. It's unreachable code in our case. [Laughter] What would my utopia be? My utopia would be a microphone where I just speak in what I want and the code comes out at the other end. Everything is correct from the very beginning. Of course, the microphone would not be able to ask me any questions about what I'd really want. I think we need to be ambitious and in terms of programming assistance – which is my vision in there – I think there are many many opportunities to increase the level of abstraction at which programmers work, to increase the amount and the quality of feedback, and I think we are nowhere near the end of these things at this point.

Jackson: Thank you Andreas Zeller. Bertrand Meyer, would you like a brief response to Patrick Cousot?[12]

Meyer: Any time something innovative is proposed, there is going to be someone who says there is no silver bullet, which is a

---

[12]Cousot made the point that we, researchers, are not modest enough. We promise too much to programmers instead of resolving their actual practical programming problems.

true proposition. It is very important not to oversell. What I've tried to present is not a solution to prevent oil rigs from capsizing or solve the problem of world hunger. It is an approach to making concurrent programming easier by raising the level of abstraction. There are a number of efforts around the world to do this. Whichever of these wins, I believe that progress in software engineering, particularly in this case progress in concurrent programming, will have to go through higher levels of abstractions. The opposition between legacy and the future has always been there and we have to go beyond it. Actually, in 1979 at ICSE in Munich, there was a panel on exactly that topic, where Barry Boehm was standing for how software engineering is and Edsger Dijkstra for what it should be. So this is not a new debate, but to a certain extent we don't have the luxury of choosing between those two goals. We need to do something for both. We have to look at the software of the past and make it better, as my neighbors on either side of me are doing, and we also need to look at what is coming afterwards.

Gurevich: Many people hold an opinion that program correctness is the main problem. I think the problem of the correctness of a program is not so difficult. In fact, I know the answer, and I already told it to Andreas Zeller. The program is not correct. [Laughter] Why not? It cannot be correct because nobody knows what correct is, at least when you think about realistic programs.

Jackson: Alright. David Parnas has a question from the audience.

David Parnas: I would like to begin by just questioning the assumptions that almost everybody has made on what we can expect from program development. Almost everybody on this panel and the other speakers have used the word real. "I work with real programs, I work with real companies. We can't expect them to hang their hat on that." And I wince every time somebody uses the word real in that way, because over history there have been all kinds of things that people said nobody real would do that, and they are routine today. It goes back to electrical engineering when

Oliver Heaviside proposed the use of certain mathematics to calculate transmission lines. It was rejected, they said nobody needs to do that, it's not real, and that people would just throw the wire down and live with it. And today nobody would dream of doing without what he proposed. When I was a fairly young assistant professor, I was told no real programmer would ever use BNF. I first wrote some simple examples with the *set* and *get* operations and was told that nobody would ever do that. All of those things I see in routine things today. And many many more, including among Eiffel programs, the use of pre- and postconditions. I started to wonder why is it that we don't demand more of the people who develop our software, instead of being so pessimistic about it and saying that nobody will ever use our techniques.

Mcycr: I have a lot of sympathy for Dave's complaint about statements of the form "no real programmer will ever do X". This has happened forever with my own work: people saying "no real programmer will ever write a contract" and of course it is completely wrong. Empirical studies show that Eiffel programmers do use contracts extensively. This being said, it does not mean that every statement of the form "no real programmer will ever do X" is wrong. You cannot infer from past mistakes that every statement of that form is false.

David Parnas: I think that it's time to start saying what can we demand and what should we not demand. I would agree that no real programmer will ever use Z. I agree that no real programmer will ever use Petri Nets. And, I could go on with a long list of things that I think no real programmer will ever use. But I'm interested in the things that we can ask and demand that real software developers do use, the same way we demand it from electrical or civil engineers.

Jackson: Thank you. You had a question?

Anonymous: Yes, my question is about correctness. We've heard a lot about preconditions, postconditions, invariants. We've had two presentations about the same problem: one in a declarative way, one in a descriptive way. Now, what I've learned in my studies is that when you have given a program in two different representations, it's undecidable to algorithmically check whether they both do the same. We proved this by reducing the problem to the termination problem. Now, I'm a little bit confused, because I never believed that the termination problem is so important. So, I would like to ask the panel what is your opinion? The main message of this seems to be that, in general, you cannot do program verification.

Leino: You can't do program verification, but that hasn't stopped me. We do engineering compromises all the time. We find workarounds for things that don't work. Concerning the duplicate representation of the preconditions, if in ten years we think back on some of the things we've discussed here, I think we'll more likely say that the precondition caught on than the postcondition. If I would ask you to specify a sorting routine, I think you would think about the postcondition of the sorting routine first: the list has to be sorted, permutation of the input. But actually the precondition is something that we would more likely stick into the code or include somewhere in the documentation as something, because the conditions can be simpler and they really help us in finding bugs. If someone called a sorting routine with a null array instead of an actual array or passes in the wrong indices, that's something we'd like to find out. And by writing this out as a precondition, there's some redundancy but it's a much simpler thing to specify in the precondition than in the middle of the running code. That also means, which is a benefit to programmers, if you get run-time checks for these things then you find the errors more quickly, namely when they occur. In a C program, if you dereference null pointers, things will definitely go wrong eventually, but that's much too late. We'd like to find out as close to the error as possible and preconditions certainly help there. So I think having the redundant representation there doesn't bother me at all.

Gurevich: I think you [directed to Anonymous] are exactly right:

in general mathematical verification is not possible. In the real world, however, verification typically does not mean mathematical verification, but engineering verification. The problem is so important and huge, and I think great progress has been achieved. If you work with toy programs then fine, but very little could have been done with huge programs. The gap between what can be done with toy programs and real programs was enormous. It is still enormous but a little bit smaller. I think more progress came actually from software engineering than from formal methods. For example, APIs, modularization. There is a movement from big size to smaller size. I think real progress has been achieved. Children typically wish they were one mile tall, imagining what great things they could do if they were giants. By the laws of physics, somebody one mile tall would collapse. Physics depends on your size. Likewise for programs, much depends on their size. My joke about knowing the answer to the correctness problem applied to huge problems where it is almost hopeless to say what correct means. Because your feature may be my bug and the other way around. There is a little bit of universal science that has been done, and I like to think abstract state machines have contributed in this respect.

Zeller: I think we, as a community, must be careful not to oversell on the notion of correctness. It is very easy to produce a program that is 100% correct. Actually it does not depend on the program at all. It just depends on the specification: you verify the correctness of the program with respect to the specification and if the latter is trivial or empty, then your program is 100% correct. The point is simply that 100% correctness does not guarantee the absence of surprises. The public confuses this normally. They think that 100% correctness amounts to absence of surprises, which is not the case. And even if you prove that your program is 100% correct with respect to a nontrivial specification, this will only be valid at some level of abstraction. But if you go down the levels of abstraction, then there will be plenty of side channels where you can then again invalidate the entire notion of correctness. So I think that, as a community, selling this 100% correctness is actually selling the wrong thing. We must show all the progress that has been made in the past, we must show the progress that has been made in different areas, in particular, the scaling from toy programs to real-life software (i.e., to multi-million lines of software), and we as a community in the past have seen lots of division: people working in symbolic verification working against people who've been working in testing. I think the best verification technique is a big mixture. Take a huge bunch of experts, put them around the software, everybody takes his favorite hammering tool and then all together we use our hammers on the software until a crack appears. That's the best we can do.

Andrey Terekhov: About toy programs and real-life programs, I am in a déjà-vu situation right now. Forty years ago there was this very popular article about the real programmer who should only write in `Fortran`. I don't remember the author of that article. In the Soviet Union we seriously debated and wondered whether that article was a joke or whether we should take it seriously. A lot were interested in correct ideas and it was written in some humorous form. The fact that today we are discussing what real means is a little bit funny, after forty years.

I also have a question for Yuri Gurevich concerning his talk. I like the approach you take for your security language. But I don't understand, I'm a mathematician as well, why you started from logic. I'm sure I can explain all your ideas in very simple words, some rights, distributions of these rights, the descending of these rights. What is this about logic? In my opinion, the fact that you are a logician by education has turned a little bit against you.

Gurevich: Good question. We really deal with a special case of distributed algorithms. Imagine a distributed algorithm and you want to prove its correctness. How can you do that? There's no global state, so what can you do? Fortunately, clever people – if I'm not mistaken, Leslie Lamport played an important role – figured out that one way to approach this problem is to formulate an invariant, which holds in the initial state and then is maintained. So you show that whatever action is performed by whatever player, the invariant is maintained. My goal was exactly along these lines. In a clinical trial example an invariant would be that the privacy of the patients is preserved. So whatever happens, privacy should be an invariant. It's not easy, nobody knows what privacy is, but you see the trend. In another situation, we looked at a fleet of nation A that has an exercise and then there are some other nations involved, some of which are less friendly than others. Here an invariant would be that whatever happens, every fleet should be notified, they should have enough information so that they don't start shooting due to surprise. Now, in each of these scenarios, success means creating and preserving the invariant. The formulation of such an invariant can only be done in logic.

Andrey Terekhov: Can you prove this privacy, in the real life?

Gurevich: We did a real-life exercise, based on `Microsoft` resource management. Here we are in charge of some resource, and other companies want this resource. You prove under relatively simple conditions (in this case) that whoever gets the resource is indeed authorized. Logic is from that point of view indispensable. In my experience, completely contrary to David Parnas's view, software engineers do logic day in and day out. They study calculus but they very rarely use it, if ever. A typical remark that a software engineer makes to me is that one language is a subset of another. Of course the languages are not sets, but the engineers don't have the logic vocabulary to epress their intent precisely. So logic is badly needed.

Anonymous: A comment from the trenches. I've worked in industry for several years now. And I'm just interested in what is the future of software engineering. What's the goal, can we hope to make everybody who writes program code a proper engineer, that is can we make them use `Eiffel` for example? I wish we could. I think it's probably an illusion, certainly a very noble one. The thing is that what's happened over the last 30 years is the democratization of the ability to write programs and to write software including very big software these days, by anybody. `Visual Basic` and `dBASE III` started it, but now anyone can go and build some giant thing with `Java` which is a terrible language, and it will get deployed and they will even get a job in a company that will pay them to do it. I think there's two kinds of people. There's a very large set of people who can't and are payed to write software, often with the worst sort of characteristics of compiling and re-compiling and hoping it works and they don't understand what they are doing. And there's a much smaller number of people who do abstract mental modelling, including design and thinking about what they are writing, rather than just pressing buttons all the time. Now even if we could democratize the wonderful things we've seen on the screen and in the talks today and yesterday, that might help. But the question is, if the vast percentage of people to whom those features are being democratized – let's say, they download the latest version of `Eclipse` and magically it got all these fantastic new tools in there – are we going to be able to make them better abstract mental designers? Because they might just sit there and keep hitting the button except that now the screen is telling them a few sort of interesting things. Maybe they will start writing the odd invariant but I really wonder, do we have to live in a two-speed world or is there really any possibility of democratizing good practice across the whole breadth of people who do write software today?

Jackson: Thank you. Bertrand Meyer has something to say.

Meyer: On undecidability – just to back up what Rustan Leino said and what Patrick Cousot also alluded to[13] – what undecidability means in practice is very simple. It means that if you have a decent prover, at least a prover with enough power, it gives you three possible answers: (i) yes, this is

---

[13]Cousot remarked that given an undecidable problem, all practical approaches to tackling it can be viewed as lacking in some respect.

correct, (ii) no, this is incorrect, or (iii) I don't know. The latter means that there has been a timeout. It's very possible that if you had waited another millisecond, you would have gotten one of the first two answers, but by definition you don't know. That's all it means in practice. It's something you have to live with.

With respect to correctness and the benefit of writing a contract, what we find in practice (and which we have published about) is that when we analyze contract violations, we actually find a very high proportion of mistakes when we analyze them manually. A human takes a look at what happened, then we find a very high proportion of cases in which the human says that actually the code was right and the contract was wrong. You can take this as an indictment of using specifications, but in fact it is not. Because the argument here is very simple. In order to have a satisfactory program – I would even go as far as saying, in order to have a program – you need to have two things. You need to have an implementation and you need to have a specification, and the two must agree. It's clear that if you only have a specification, it doesn't solve your problem. What's not clear to most people, but which is equally true, is that if you have an implementation and no specification, it is in fact just as bad because you then have a program that does something and you don't know what it does. So what you need is both. And then when you find a mistake, by which I mean a discrepancy between the two, it doesn't matter that much actually whether the discrepancy is in the implementation or in the specification, because if the implementation is intuitively right but you've not been able to specify correctly the real intent – the psycho-analysis so to speak of the programmer's intent – then we have something wrong any way.

Jackson: Back to the question of democratization.

Leino: You mentioned the dissemination of good practice, and I think that's a theme that came up a number of times today and yesterday. I think it would be wonderful if we could get engineers who think that they are good engineers to write good example programs. It could be a snippet of code or something, hang it on a blog somewhere and say this is a good style for writing this kind of program or algorithm. If we could do that for a number of examples, or build a collection of those things, it would also be wonderful to give some correctness arguments, be they informal or formalized so that we can say why this is a good practice, why this sort of pattern works. Maybe we could change software engineering by doing more such peer-to-peer teaching.

Anonymous: There's a lot of great stuff out there. It's a question of making it easier to get the great stuff.

Leino: I would have thought that we do have a number of sources, but nevertheless it has come up now, just in the last two days, that people are wishing for such good places to look for good code. It probably means that we have room for doing it much more.

Zeller: We also need to understand that programming now frequently happens at a scale that we thought would have been impossible 20 years ago. We have such powerful frameworks, such powerful tools. Programming in many aspects today is not so much about designing algorithms, it is actually also not so much about thinking about pre- and postconditions (or at least pre- and postconditions in terms of states as they used to be), but it's more like: How do I make this part interact with this other part? How do I put this together? How do I make sure that I have thought of every single interaction that can take place? This is a level of programming that is very much different from classical engineering, that is a level of programming that indeed is amenable to people who have no formal training – it is like putting a Lego box together – but the devil is in the details. Think about user interfaces, yes you put these together, but have you thought about people who only have a keyboard and no mouse? Have you thought about internationalization? All these issues, all these little details that make so much work, they are so important for coming up with good usability, this becomes evident when you put these objects together. These are properties that cannot be expressed in terms of pre- and postconditions. So we need other ways to express and enforce such rules.

Anonymous: I have a question about the future of software which concerns myself and my own future. I have to deal with parallel programming and I find, indeed, that parallel programming becomes easier and easier. One thing I am interested in is whether I will in the future need to know about the hardware architecture. Things like implicit locking in the cache lines, or can I hope that there will be abstraction instruments that will just do everything right for me. Or shall I have to take some verification tools of profilers that will show that really what I am doing is what I want to have?

Meyer: We are in a transitory period at the moment. What you are saying is absolutely correct. Apart from the approach I've presented, there are others trying to go in the same direction of abstracting from the details of the concurrency architectures that we have: hardware and operating system. Because it is impossible, really, to program significant concurrent applications with the tools we have. First, they are very difficult to use and then, once you've written your program, it is difficult to sleep at night: you never know if there's going to be a data race or a deadlock. So, the future inevitably requires higher-level abstractions; I presented one which I hope will be widely used. There are other developments like lock-free data structures. The general idea is the same: free programmers from the details. As I said, we are in a temporary situation and it is just not possible today for a programmer to ignore the gory details, in particular, with respect to performance as I believe Patrick Cousot mentioned earlier[14].

Gurevich: Here's my crystal ball. I think we need something, like physics needed quantum physics. Let me explain why

---

[14]Cousot pointed out that many programmers will not trade control of program performance for a higher level of abstraction. The latter is only acceptable if it, too, provides the programmer with a handle (of some kind) on performance.

I make this analogy. What distinguishes quantum physics from normal physics? In normal physics we have intuition to support what we understand. In quantum physics nobody has intuition; all we have is a mathematical apparatus which tells us how it is. Coming back to comprehension, we are sequential. It is almost impossible for us to comprehend parallel processes. Eventually I am sure we will solve this problem, but even when it will be solved, it will be hard for us to comprehend, we will not have simple intuition like physicists don't have intuition for quantum physics. So I don't know whether it will happen soon enough for you, but I'm sure it will be solved, and the solution probably will be strange. Think of machine learning and such sorts of things; these techniques will help us deal with parallelism in a way that is hard for us to comprehend.

Jackson: Thank you very much. That has to be the end, I'm sorry about that, but we do have to leave this room. The coffee is waiting outside. Let's give a big thank you to the panel.

LONELY SCHOLAR™
SCIENTIFIC BOOKS

Don't miss our upcoming publications.
www.lonelyscholar.com

Conversations

Pluralism in Software Engineering:
Turing Award Winner Peter Naur Explains
October 2011

Books

Dijkstra's Rallying Cry for Generalization
scheduled release date: early 2012

www.ingramcontent.com/pod-product-compliance
Lightning Source LLC
La Vergne TN
LVHW052323060326
832902LV00023B/4576